EGYPTIAN WALL-PAINTINGS

From Tombs and Temples

FONTANA UNESCO ART BOOKS

Egyptian
Wall-Paintings

FROM TOMBS AND TEMPLES

Christiane Desroches-Noblecourt

COLLINS · UNESCO

Egyptian painting may be said to have begun in pre-historic times when the first craftsman thought of chewing the end of a reed and using it to draw human figures, animals and plants on his white or pink coloured pottery. The notion of decoration, which goes back to neolithic times, gradually took form and developed, but neither the general trends in drawing nor the basic themes expressed were to stray very far from their original inspiration.

The word "painting" usually conjures up portraiture, the evocation of an atmosphere or the narration of an event. But Egyptian painting must not be regarded in exactly this way. In early times the same holds for neighbouring countries on the eastern Mediterranean. Drawings were undoubtedly made as expressive as possible, for they had a meaning, but the meaning was what really mattered. For thousands of years the painter was simply a decorator whose personality took second place to what he had to colour or express. Gifted though he might be, the artist-craftsman could not give free rein to his fancy. Attitudes, the choice of colours and the rendering of shapes were all pre-defined. The study and comparison of similar themes treated in different regions of Egypt and in widely different periods, show to what extent relief, drawing and painting conform to an absolute law. Designed to complement each other, these techniques remained always subordinate to decoration, which was actually a very much enlarged form of writing. We have only to close our eyes to the details which

5

Deir el-Bahari: temple of Queen Hatshepsut.

Entrance to underground tomb in the Valley of Kings.

decorate these painted scenes, imagine them on a smaller scale, and we can see strips of diverse hieroglyphs much the same as those we find in the majestic friezes composing the texts of certain noblemen's tombs and the ornamental inscriptions on temples.

Rich hieroglyphs of this kind are to be found even earlier than the magnificent funeral texts carved and painted along the side of the vault of King Unas' pyramid at Sakkara. And at the end of the pharaonic dynasties they are still recalled by the hieroglyphs made out of multicoloured glass pastes set in the wood of the mummy-shaped sarcophagus of the High Priest Petosiris. If we are to consider outlines only we have the linear hieroglyphs such as those used by the scribes, and even by Egyptologists in our own day.

In classical times, as soon as the support permitted, this extraordinary, enlarged pictographic writing took the form of very fine incisions on quality limestone. It was also sculpted in hard granite or thinly drawn on various Nilotic sandstones. Painting was usually introduced to heighten the effect and to add a realistic note; details were left to the painter or decorator to fill in. But even before the engraver set to work, the painter made a rough outline of the design on the wall. Traces left in unfinished tombs bear witness to the sure touch of the painter. The craftsman often drew to scale, which enabled him not only to enlarge a scene of which he had a small model but also, and mainly, to give the subjects the proportions laid down in the canon.

Thus painting was the necessary complement to engraving, a means of making it more expressive and evocative, of endowing the work with magical life. All ancient Egyptian art was coloured. The ordinary people painted on poor quality wood, pottery or stone; the great commissioned funeral effigies with polychrome effects and iridescent reliefs for their tombs; kings had their burial chambers decorated with remarkable paintings in which they figured in colour alongside the gods and spirits; temple walls were embellished throughout with gold leaf and painted reliefs; the hieroglyphs on the obelisks were studded with lapis-lazuli. The jewelry placed in the tombs on mummies of ordinary people, nobles and pharaohs was supposed to keep the deceased warm by the powerful radiations emanating from the stones or coloured glass pastes with which it was set. Furniture, too, was inlaid or painted. To earthly life and to eternal life colour was as vital as any other element able to confer existence and immortality.

Though colour was an essential factor, as we may see from the prescriptions given in magic papyri for making amulets, it was not to be used indiscriminately. A particular amulet had to be made with a particular stone whose colour gave full force to the charm. Many of the surviving painted inscriptions indicate that the same held true for hieroglyphs. The essentials of these strict injunctions are to be found in decorative painting as well. For instance, women's skin is always painted light or pinkish yellow whereas men's skin is red ochre. The only exception was the goddess Hathor who, according to the law, had a skin as dark as that of a man. Backgrounds are white — less frequently, yellow. The only break with tradition was in the Amarna period and the years immediately preceding and following that era of rapid evolution. It took the form of a search for new colours, a freedom in the expression of movement and a verisimilitude in the representation of forms which had never been attained before. Even then, however, the artist did not break completely with tradition; he remained bound by the artistic conventions established "in the time of the Gods".

These conventions are now famous and bound up with the whole conception of Egyptian art: the body was a synthesis of the various elements of which it consists: the lines went off at different angles but appeared "logical"; the face was shown in profile, the bust from the front, the hips slightly turned and the legs viewed from the side. In this way shapes were clearer and more easily recognizable. Essential planes were not diminished and both shoulders were visible. The eye was depicted looking at the spectator, and though facial expressions were not accentuated, at least the most vital part of the face was evoked — with no concern naturally, for perspective. Consequently it appears incomplete or distorted though the essential features were

9

Tomb of Queen Nefertari. The celestial bull and seven cows.
Detail. Nineteenth dynasty.

The fluted columns of the T-shaped temple, as restored, and the Step Pyramid at Saqqarah.

11

kept intact. This law may be observed in the two-dimensional rendering of shapes from the very beginning of figured decoration.

On pre-dynastic vases only black and white were used. The oldest decorative mural painting we know was found in a tomb of Upper Egypt dating from the dawn of history, before the advent of writing. It is the one from Hierakonpolis (Cairo Museum), and in it yellow and red ochres, blacks and whites predominate. Already the design was sure and basically nothing further was to be added. As early as the Old Kingdom (2778-2263) the technique of mural design and painting was fixed. In cases where the support — that is the stone on which the decoration was to appear — was not satisfactory the craftsman did not sculpt the traditional scenes; he simply covered the poor stone or brick surface with plaster and painted the scene in distemper on a white ground — occasionally yellow, as mentioned above. He used natural colors pulverized and diluted with water and gum which helped them to stick to the support. (It is claimed that egg yoke and encaustic were included, for the colours were intensified by heat).

The possible existence of a very thin covering varnish is a moot point, and anyhow it does not appear before the xixth dynasty. Yellows and brick reds were obtained from natural desert ochres, white from chalk or lime. Lamp-black also was used: this soot was always very fragile and did not adhere well to any kind of support. Blues and greens were extracted from calcined mixtures with a cobalt base for blue, a copper base for green. The ivth dynasty gave rise to some very original experiments. The scenes instead of being painted over reliefs or on plaster were studded with coloured pastes embedded in the limestone. Short-lived, this technique was used at Meidum.

What then was the purpose of this decoration which must have been iridescent and dynamic, unlike the statuary which was always more sober? As painting it developed on the walls of temples and tombs, where it complemented reliefs, or even replaced them when the support was too poor to provide a satisfactory surface. Painting then came into its own. Though still subordinated to a predetermined theme it had wider scope. The significance of temple decorations is no longer in dispute. They had a theological meaning and served to explain the ceremonies that took place within the sanctuary; they illustrated the aspirations of the clergy and the concept of the divine right of kings. Tomb decorations, on the other hand, still give rise to controversy and the problem will doubtless not be elucidated until agreement is reached on the Egyptian conception of the after-life.

However there was an increasing trend for the scenes to be painted not so much just to please the eye of the visitor to the funeral chamber as to help the deceased in his efforts to attain eternal life after a superterrestrial rebirth. This would explain the close similarity of inspiration in the themes painted on the walls of tombs — "mastabas" of the Old Kingdom, "hypogea" carved out of the rock face in Middle Egypt in the time of the Amenemhats or the Sesostris, or the burial places in the Libyan chain west of Thebes in the New Kingdom. It is beyond doubt that the rendering of shapes underwent considerable evolution during these different periods, together with the interpretation of the themes and the technique of drawing, but the message, in some intangible way, remains ever the same and objective observers are left wondering as to the meaning of it all.

In any case these observations cannot be understood without very careful study of the themes. These remained essentially the same from the beginnings of Egyptian art until the fall of the last Pharaoh, even when they were transposed to minor art objects or certain temple walls of the later period. The respect they apparently commanded gives them their full significance.

Mostly rural, they appeared in the Old Kingdom on the walls of built-up tombs, or "mastabas". They included sowing, plowing, harvesting, flax gathering, the arrival of livestock, the fattening of certain creatures such as grees, cranes, oryx and even hyenas, whose meat was apparently relished by the Egyptians. Scribes are seen supervising the arrival of cattle or the storage of grain. All these activities served to prepare the regular funeral offering necessary for

Tomb of Anhurkhawi. The barge of the Sun. Among the passengers are Thot the ibis-headed god, the Sun-god, whose head is replaced by a scarab, and the god Hu. Ramessid period. Nineteenth dynasty.

Temple of Queen Hatshepsut. Funeral chapel of Thutmosis I.
Frieze of Uraeus and fragmentary inscription. Eighteenth dynasty.

supplying the tables from which the deceased could get his nourishment — real or symbolic — for the desired after-life. But it does not seem certain that this offering had a "projection" in the after life in any literal sense. The symbol, or allegorical evocation, whose message had to be transposed in the transcendental sphere, was certainly an essential factor in the choice of figures. The purpose of the agricultural and farm scenes was the offering to the deceased: the funeral banquet scene showed to what extent it was necessary to help in the perpetuation of this rite. Musicians and dancers enlivened the banquet while contributing through mime and rhythmic harmony to the ritual of the funeral offering.

On the walls of the tombs all the requisites for fulfilling the rites were depicted first in the process of manufacture and again in their finished state — boats for pilgrimages, water tournaments or wild-fowling, chairs and coffers for the burial chambers, weapons for hunting exploits, and even the small statues of the deceased. Considerable space was devoted to hunting scenes — netting birds in trees or aquatic birds in the marshes. Sometimes desert animals were shown, pursued by dogs across sand dunes scattered with a few meagre spiny plants. Many scenes represented draw-net fishing in swamps or ponds. The light barge of the deceased seems to glide as if enchanted through the papyrus thickets, against a veritable curtain of papyrus. The deceased, in a standing position, occasionally seizes the stalks with both hands and shakes them. The noise was supposed to attract the goddess Hathor, patron of the necropolis, who came to seek the deceased. With these themes we enter the strictly sepuchral realm, if we can be said to have left it. We are now reasonably sure that the netting of aquatic birds and fish symbolised the annihilation of the enemies of the deceased, that is, of the larvae that might have prevented him finally reaching the land of the blessed.

Similarly the oft-repeated scene of the hippopotamus hunt, depicted in an aquatic setting, with crocodiles ready to fall on their prey at the bottom of the river and the deceased valiantly brandishing his javelin, actually represented the combat with the Evil One. Magic forbade representation of the demon, who was evoked in the form of a noxious animal destroyed by kings at the dawn of history and later — in pictorial form — by noblemen, then burghers, in order to gain immortality after passing through ordeals and trials.

Evil had to be vanquished but the deceased had to be sure of regaining his immortal soul. So he first hunted marsh birds with a boomerang, breaking the necks and wings of the wild ducks which embodied the spirit of disorder. Sometimes peaceful birds or animals were used as decoys — the Nile goose, mongooses or the familiar cat — and helped to hunt wildfowl amongst the reeds and papyrus.

All these many-hued fluttering wings of birds suddenly disturbed, the young ones alarmed in their nests, the butterflies hovering over the marshes and the hunters' cat drunk with joy at the prospect of the carnage, were the essential elements in a decorative theme which, with variations in detail, was repeated for over three thousand years. Yet in its composition, the distribution of volumes and the interplay of colours, it nearly always reached the standard of great art. The marsh scene was always included when tombs were decorated. One side showed the deceased in his skiff made of papyrus preparing to throw a boomerang at the birds flushed from the marshes. The other side showed a fishing scene. But here again it was a symbolic evocation. The deceased was shown harpooning two fish whose size was grossly exaggerated, no doubt for the sake of the theme. They were always of the same species, a *lates niloticus* and a *tilapia nilotica*, or, from the New Kingdom on, two *tilapia*. We now know that these fish symbolized the two forms of the mummified deceased ready to be born again from the primordial ocean which would give him immortality, or, in the case of the two *tilapia*, the two forms of the reborn deceased, representing his previous "soul" and his new "soul". The same symbol was taken up by all the religions of the East and Near East and is exemplified in the *ichthys* of the early Christians.

Such complex symbols were not uncommon, as we now

Tomb of Rameses I. Khepri, the scarab-headed sun-god.
Nineteenth dynasty.

Tomb of Prince Amenherkhepeshef in the Valley of Queens.
King Rameses III, the Prince's father, leads the Goddess Isis
by the hand. Twentieth dynasty.

discover on closer study. But at least the edge of this heavy veil will have been lifted and the reader will understand that the arts of agricultural, though not primitive civilizations, expressed magical concepts while existing in their own right as artistic creations of the highest value. Employed simply as a means of expression, they attained their aims to perfection.

Mural decorations were always arranged in horizontal strips or friezes and the various scenes were superimposed one above the other, as, for example, the famous Meidum geese painted directly on plaster (Cairo Museum) or the reliefs on the mastabas at Gizeh, Sakkara or on any necropolis of the Old or Middle Kingdom. Although the themes were often similar, since the artist was obliged to revert to them, he usually showed his originality in treating them according to his own fancy. He even added humorous details and anecdotes of everyday life which made of his works real genre paintings whose religious or magical significance we can sometimes forget.

In the middle Kingdom (2065-1785) the tombs were less rich in painted reliefs, the scenes being mainly painted in distemper directly on a whitened wall without any relief work. To the traditional themes were added some new elements, such as fabulous animals and funeral spirits in a purely agricultural setting or such topical scenes as the training of soldiers in the defence of their country and its territories, the scaling of citadels or battles with the Nubians. These often fratricidal struggles also symbolized victory over the adversary in the spiritual sphere. The big marsh hunting compositions often occupied a whole wall. The hippopotamus hunt extended over several horizontal strips.

In the New Kingdom (1580-1085 the tendency to expand the list of themes became even stronger. Whole compositions were set forth on the walls of temples. They are still to be found at Amarna on the walls of the tombs of the eastern necropolis of Akhetaton. A new expressionism marked the paintings in pastel tones and off colours which decorated the houses and palaces of the heretic period. Birds are seen flying and alighting amidst exuberant vegetation rendered with much naturalistic detail. There was no longer any question of making a synthesis of forms or expressing in paint the elements of gigantic writing. Figures were linked with one anotheer and there was an interplay of the various components of the scene which enabled them all to co-exist on the same plane. Neutral tones made possible certain innovations such as the symphony in reds in which two little princesses appear as though on a cameo.

But a very advanced stage had been reached in the slow development of styles even before this period. While still observing the essential rules of drawing, painters took liberties and tried to go back to nature. They introduced and stressed a variety of naturalistic details. Though their works gained in flexibility, they still remained within certain limits. Painters excelled in showing two almost identical figures very close together in different poses. The two profiles seem the same, but close examination reveals a multitude of details which give each its individuality.

Egyptian painting reached its greatest heights of expression during the xvⅢth dynasty. One has only to compare the charmingly evocative and elegant though stiff scenes of Rekhmara's tomb (Thutmosis III) with those of the tomb of Nakht or of Jeserkareseneb (Thutmosis IV) to realize to what extent decorative painting had suddenly been emancipated from its subsidiary role and had acquired, if only momentarily, the status of an independent art, an expression of human feeling. Delicate faces are individualized by means of minute details; bodies are revealed through transparent and elegant drapery; movements are graceful and colours much more finely differentiated. Even animals' fur is shaded off. The same freedom and casual charm may sometimes be found on Theban walls of this period: The artists' studies made on *ostraca*, or chips of limestone, are still to be seen.

At the beginning of the Ramessid period, which came after the Amarma period, tomb decoration was often free and fanciful with a tendency to realism such as prevailed before the great heresy. But artistic inspiration was very soon sacrificed once again to metaphysical considerations: the magical scenes expressed in little genre-paintings of everyday life gave way to monumental religious decorations. The walls of private chapels more frequently bore the "vignettes" which on a much smaller scale decorated tomb papyri. From the very beginning of the New Kingdom royal tombs were decorated in that way, but this great decorative art was replaced by bright and even garish coloured scenes. Postures were stiff and unrealistic and evocation gave way to pure decoration. The complex picture degenerated into something almost resembling wallpaper. However the best craftsmen to be found in the Nile Valley were always called upon for the wall engravings in royal tombs. The tomb of Queen Nefertari, beloved wife of Ramses II, is the most characteristic example and the last real masterpiece. This type of ornamentation imposed on the artist a limited choice of religious subjets and a conventional arrangement which did not leave room for imaginative treatment. The charm and majesty of pure lines and exquisitely blended colours still combine to make a sanctuary befitting a queen. For the first time flesh tones are well rendered; the queen's skin is shadowed and her earrings are brought nicely into relief by the colours. Despite his restricted compass, the artist seems to have treated the Queen's face as a portrait. Careful study reveals that individual differences were suggested by minute details. And so, just after it had freed itself from its subordinate and narrative role, Egyptian painting was once again to lose all that it had achieved and all that it had learned to express with such ease. This painting had, however, foreshadowed — and even achieved — standards which, after many centuries, artists were to rediscover and in their turn surpass, raising this technique to the dignity of an independent art.

Tomb of Sennefer. The wife of the deceased, the Lady Merit,
offering a jar full of nard (?). Eighteenth dynasty.

CHRONOLOGY OF ANCIENT EGYPT

PERIODS	DYNASTIES	DATES B. C.
Old Kingdom		
Thinite Period	I & II	3197-2778
Memphite Period	III-V	2778-2423 circa
First Intermediary Period	VI-XI	2423-2065 circa
Middle Kingdom		
First Theban Empire	XI-XII	2065-1785
Second Intermediary Period (Hyksos conquest)	XIII-XVII	1785-1580
New Kingdom	XVIII-XX	1580-1085
Late Period		
Priest kings	XXI	1085-950
Libyan kings	XXI-XXIII	950-730
Saitic kings	XXIV	730-715
Ethiopian kings	XXV	715-663
Saitic kings (called Saitic Period)	XXVI	663-525
Persian rule and last of the Egyptian kings	XXVII-XXX	525-332
Ptolemic and Roman Period		332 to the Arab invasion

ILLUSTRATIONS

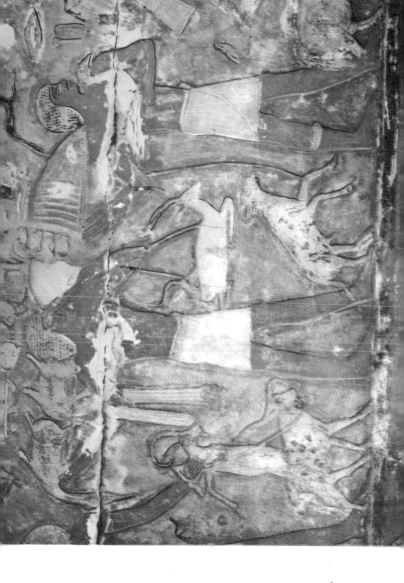

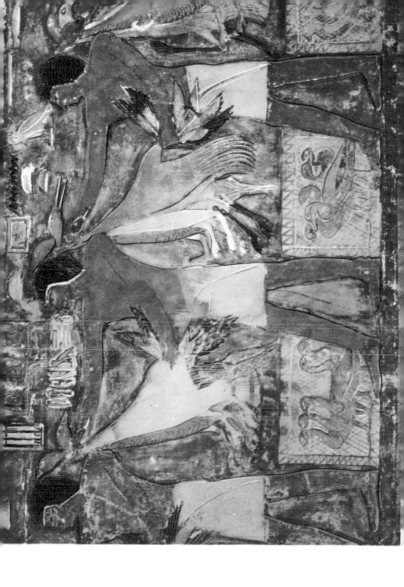

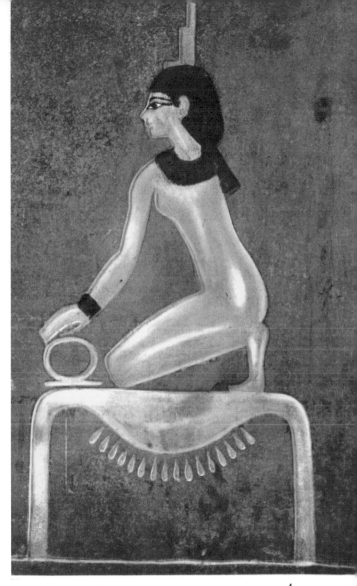

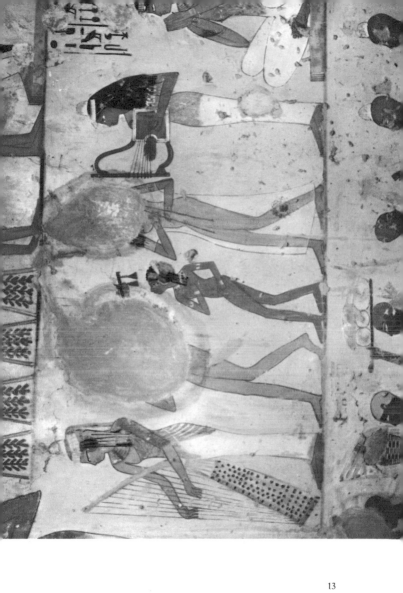

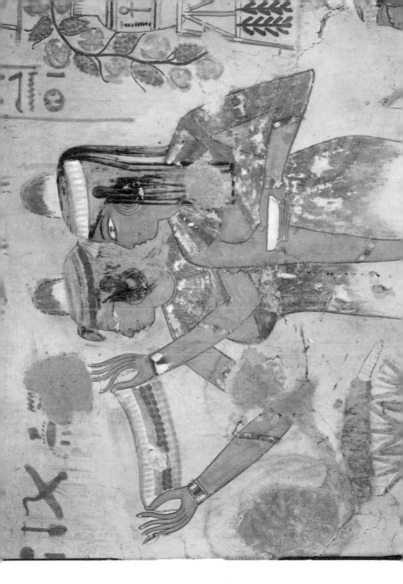

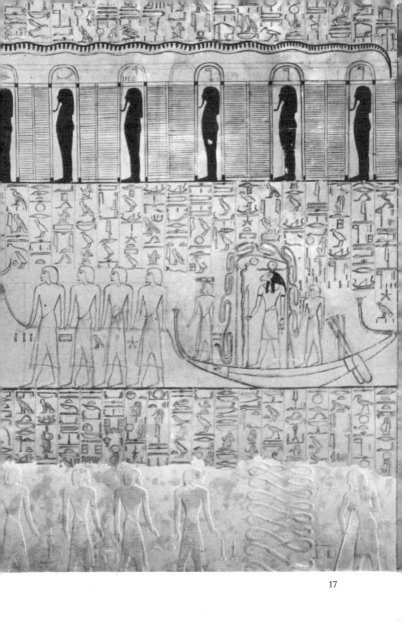